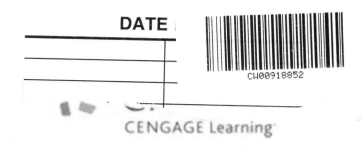
Novels for Students, Volume 15

Project Editor: David Galens

Editorial: Sara Constantakis, Anne Marie Hacht, Michael L. LaBlanc, Ira Mark Milne, Pam Revitzer, Jennifer Smith, Daniel Toronto, Carol Ullman Permissions: Debra Freitas, Shalice Shah-Caldwell

Manufacturing: Stacy Melson

Imaging and Multimedia: Lezlie Light, Kelly A. Quin, Luke Rademacher Product Design: Michelle DiMercurio, Pamela A. E. Galbreath, Michael Logusz © 2002 by Gale. Gale is an imprint of The Gale group, Inc., a division of Cengage Learning Inc.

of the editors or publisher. Errors brought to the
attention of the publisher and verified to the
satisfaction of the publisher will be corrected in
future editions.

ISBN 0-7876-4898-1
ISSN 1094-3552

Printed in the United States of America
10 9 8 7 6 5 4 3 2 1

A Clockwork Orange

Anthony Burgess 1962

Introduction

Published in 1962, Anthony Burgess's *A Clockwork Orange* is set in the future and narrated by fifteen-year-old Alex in Nadsat—a language invented by Burgess and comprised of bits of Russian, English, and American slang, rhyming words, and "gypsy talk". The British edition of the novel contains three sections divided into seven chapters, for a total of twenty-one chapters, the number symbolizing adulthood. The original American edition, however, contains only twenty chapters, as the publisher cut the last chapter because he felt it was too sentimental. A new American edition came out in 1987 with the expunged chapter restored. Although

Burgess claimed that the book is neither his favorite nor his best, *A Clockwork Orange* helped to establish his international reputation, owing largely to Stanley Kubrick's film adaptation of it in 1971. The novel's title alludes to the Cockney saying, "as queer as a clockwork orange," which means that something can appear to be natural, but on the inside it is actually artificial. Burgess's novel explores issues such as the relation between evil and free will, and the state's role in human affairs.

Burgess, a self-avowed anarchist, visited Leningrad (in what was then the Soviet Union) in 1961 and was appalled at the degree to which the communist state controlled people's lives. He based the character of Alex and his band of thugs ("droogs" in Nadsat) on Russian and British gangs of the 1950s and 1960s. The Russian *stilyaqi*, or style-boys, reminded Burgess of the teddy boys, a macho British youth subculture. "Inspiration" for a violent scene in the novel stems from an incident in 1943 when a group of AWOL (absent without leave) American soldiers attacked and raped Burgess's then-pregnant wife, Llewela Isherwood Jones, in London, killing their unborn child. Though his wife died more than two decades later, Burgess attributed her subsequent alcoholism and death from cirrhosis of the liver to that incident.

Author Biography

John Anthony Burgess Wilson was born in 1917 in Manchester, England, to Joseph, a cashier and pub pianist, and Elizabeth (Burgess) Wilson. His mother and sister died of the flu in 1919, and Burgess was raised by a maternal aunt, and later by his stepmother. He studied in England at Xaverian College and Manchester University, from where he graduated in 1940 with a degree in English language and literature, though his chief passion was music. After serving in the Royal Army Medical Corps during World War II, Burgess pursued a career in education, teaching at Birmingham University and Banbury Grammar School and working for the Ministry of Education.

In 1959, while an education officer in Brunei, Borneo, doctors diagnosed Burgess with a cerebral tumor, giving him a year to live. It was then he began writing in earnest, steadily turning out novels, columns, and reviews. He dropped his first and last names because he felt it was inappropriate for a member of the British Colonial Service to publish under his own name. Burgess did not die within the year, and continued writing at a torrid pace, churning out eleven novels between 1960 and 1964 alone.

In 1962 Burgess's novel *A Clockwork Orange* was published, a satirical work detailing the violent exploits of a futuristic teenage gang and its

Beethoven-loving leader, Alex. The novel satirizes psychologist B. F. Skinner's theories of human behavior and the welfare state. Stanley Kubrick's adaptation of the novel into a feature film in 1971 won Burgess numerous new readers and secured the novel's reputation as one of the most controversial in English literature. Unfortunately for Burgess, because he was financially strapped, he had sold the film rights to *A Clockwork Orange* for just $500 (U.S.) and received less than $3,000 (U.S.) in payments after the film's release.

Burgess edited and published numerous books after *A Clockwork Orange* including novels, screenplays, autobiographies, critical studies, documentaries, and an opera. None of them ever achieved the degree of notoriety that *A Clockwork Orange* received. These works include *The Novel Today* (1963); *The Eve of Saint Venus* (1964); *Language Made Plain* (1964); *Here Comes Everybody: A Study of James Joyce's Fiction* (1965); *Tremor of Intent* (1966); *The Novel Now* (1967); *Earthly Powers* (1980), winner of the Prix du Meilleur Livre Etranger in 1981; *Enderby's Dark Lady* (1984); and his autobiography *Little Wilson and Big God* (1986). Burgess's last novel, *Byrne: A Novel*, written in ottava rima (a stanza of eight lines of heroic verse with a rhyme scheme of *abababcc*), was published posthumously in 1995.

Almost all of Burgess's novels explore the conflicts between good and evil, the spirit and the flesh. Born a Catholic in Protestant England, Burgess believed that although people are born depraved, they retain the capacity to choose, and it is this capacity that makes human beings human. A fellow of the Royal Society of Literature, Burgess died of cancer in London, England, in 1993.

First Section

    A Clockwork Orange opens with Alex, the main character of the novel, and his droogs, Dim, Pete, and Georgie, drinking drug-laced milk at the Korova Milkbar. After leaving the Milkbar, the four commit what is to be the first in a string of "ultraviolent" acts, savagely beating up an old man carrying library books and destroying his books. Next, the group comes across a rival gang in a warehouse. Billyboy, the leader, and his five droogs are raping a young devotchka (girl), and Alex's crew attacks them, beating them back until the millicents (police) arrive.

    Alex and his gang next come to a house with the word "HOME" on the front gate. This marks a turn in the novel towards the fabular (fantastical), and away from the realistic. After telling the woman answering the door that his friend is sick and he needs to use her phone, Alex breaks into the house with his gang, now wearing masks. They viciously beat the woman's husband and pillage the house, then gang rape the woman. The man, F. Alexander, is a writer working on a book called *A Clockwork Orange*, which Alex calls a "gloopy" title. The book critiques the welfare state and government oppression of civil liberties. The droogs destroy the book. (This scene echoes an event from 1943 in

Burgess's own life, when his wife was raped and brutalized by a gang of American soldiers.)

After returning to the Milkbar, Alex hits Dim for ridiculing a woman singing opera at the bar. Georgie and Pete side with Dim, Pete remarking, "If the truth is known, Alex, you shouldn't have given old Dim that uncalled-for tolchock [blow] ... if it had been me you'd given it to you'd have to answer." Alex returns to his parents' flat and falls asleep masturbating while listening to Beethoven. In the morning, his Post-Corrective Advisor, P. R. Deltoid, visits him, warning Alex that one day the police will catch him if he continues with his antics. After Deltoid leaves, Alex visits a music store, where he picks up two ten-year-old girls, brings them back to his apartment, plies them with liquor, and rapes them.

At the Milkbar, Pete, Georgie, and Dim convince Alex that they need to rob a larger house. Alex goes along with the plan, to show he is a good "brother" and leader. That night, they break into the house of an elderly wealthy woman who is feeding her cats. She fights with Alex, and he knocks her out with one of her statues. When Alex tries to escape after hearing the police sirens, Dim hits him with his chain, knocking him out. The police arrive and arrest Alex, as Georgie, Pete, and Dim abandon him. The police take him to a cell, where he is visited by Deltoid, who spits in his face. Alex later learns that the old woman he fought with has died of a heart attack. "That was everything," Alex says. "I'd done the lot, now. And me still only fifteen."

Media Adaptations

- *A Clockwork Orange* (1971) was adapted as a film by director Stanley Kubrick and stars Malcolm McDowell, Patrick Magee, Adrienne Corri, Aubrey Morris, and James Marcus. It is available in both VHS and DVD format.

- Harper Audio publishes an audiocassette of Burgess reading from *A Clockwork Orange*.

Second Section

The second section, chapters eight through fourteen, describes Alex's life in the "staja" (state penitentiary), after he is sentenced to fourteen years there. A model prisoner—despite killing a fellow prisoner who had been making sexual advances towards him—Alex makes fast friends with the chaplain, who allows him to listen to classical music on the chapel stereo. Prison officials and the Minister of the Interior offer Alex the opportunity to undergo Ludovico's Technique, an experimental treatment that guarantees his release from prison and ensures he will never return, and Alex agrees. Burgess models the idea of Ludovico's Technique on the work of B. F. Skinner. Skinner, a mid-twentieth-century behavioral psychologist, wanted to build a society based on a system of rewards and punishments. He believed that human behavior could be conditioned, once people learned to associate "good" behavior with the pleasure of the reward they received for it, and associate "bad" behavior with the pain of punishment. These methods were used for a time on juvenile delinquents and retarded children. Skinner outlines his ideas in his book *Beyond Freedom and Dignity*.

For two weeks, Alex is given injections of a drug that makes him physically ill whenever he witnesses violent acts. His eyelids clamped open, Alex is forced to watch films packed with scenes of torture, rape, and beating. After being shown a film detailing Nazi atrocities from World War II, with Beethoven's Fifth Symphony as its sound track, Alex develops an aversion to both violence and Beethoven, whose music he loves. At the conclusion of the treatment, Alex is paraded before a panel of prison and state officials, during which time he grovels in front of a tormentor taunting him to fight and is sickened by his own lustful response to a beautiful woman. Alex has been stripped of free will to choose his actions, and Dr. Brodsky pronounces him fit for release from prison.

Third Section

In the third section, Alex becomes a victim. In his absence, Alex's parents have taken a boarder, Joe, so Alex is forced to the streets, where he encounters the people he victimized in the first section. He is being beaten by a group of old men in the Public Biblio (library), one of whom Alex and his gang had beaten before. Alex is then "rescued" by three policemen, two of whom turn out to be Billy boy and Dim. The government had recruited the two in its efforts to use society's criminal elements for its own repressive purposes. Billy boy and Dim take Alex out to the country, beat him, and leave him for dead. Alex then wanders through a village and comes upon the house with "HOME" written on the gate. F. Alexander, the writer beaten by Alex earlier, recognizes Alex from the newspaper and takes him in, planning to use him in a campaign to "dislodge this overbearing government."

While Alexander and his liberal friends brainstorm how to use Alex as an example of government repression, the writer recognizes Alex as the person who beat him up and raped his wife a few years ago. With his friends' help, Alexander locks Alex in an apartment and plays classical music, Otto Skadelig's Symphony Number Three, driving Alex into a suicidal frenzy because of the sickness and pain he feels listening to the music. Alex jumps out the window, but does not die. He awakens in the hospital, his love for violence restored. Mean-while, the Minister of the Interior visits Alex, telling him that Alexander and his friends have been imprisoned, and offering Alex a well-paying job in exchange for his support of the government.

In the last chapter, Alex is back at the Korova Milkbar, this time with a new group of droogs, who resemble the old group. Although they engage in ultraviolent acts, Alex says that he mostly gives orders and watches. He is "old" now, eighteen. He meets one of his former gang members, Pete, who is married and works for an insurance company, and Alex begins to fantasize about also being married and having children. "Youth must go, ah yes," he says. "But youth is only being in a way like it might be an animal."

Characters

Alex

Alex is the fifteen-year-old narrator and protagonist of the novel. Like his "droogs," Dim, Georgie, and Pete, he speaks in Nadsat. He is witty, charming, intelligent, violent, sadistic, and totally without remorse for his actions. He leads his gang on crime sprees, raping, beating, and pillaging, and becomes upset when his gang does not engage in their crimes with style. Alex's love of music, particularly Beethoven, marks him as an aesthete, and this attitude carries over to the way he "performs" his violent acts, often dancing. His attitude towards others is primarily ironic; he calls his victims "brother" and speaks as if with a perpetual smirk. The extent of Alex's evil nature is evident in his fantasies. For example, he dreams about nailing Jesus to the cross. Authorities are perplexed as to how Alex became the way he is. His guidance counselor, P. R. Deltoid, asks him, "You've got a good home here, good loving parents, you've got not too bad of a brain. Is it some devil that crawls inside you?" Alex remains his evil self, even after two years in prison and Ludovico's Technique, though he behaves differently. In the last chapter, however, Alex matures and begins to weary of his violent ways, fantasizing about having a wife and children. Burgess notes that among other things, Alex's name suggests nobleness, Alexander meaning "leader of men."

F. Alexander

F. Alexander—whom Alex describes as "youngish" and with horn-rimmed glasses the first time he sees him, and "a shortish veck in middle age, thirty, forty, fifty" the second time he sees him —is a liberal and a writer, outraged at the government's repression of individual liberties. Ironically, he is writing a book called *A Clockwork Orange*, which addresses "[t]he attempt to impose upon man, a creature of growth and capable of sweetness ... laws and conditions appropriate to a mechanical creation." In the novel's first section, Alex breaks into Alexander's house, where he and his gang beat him and viciously rape his wife. Beaten almost to death by Billyboy and Georgie in the third section, Alex winds up back at Alexander's house. At first, Alexander wants to use Alex as an example of the government's repressive policies, and he befriends Alex, who considers him "kind protecting and like motherly." However, when Alexander realizes that Alex is the person responsible for beating him and raping his wife a few years past, he plots revenge. Along with his liberal friends, Alexander locks Alex up in an apartment, and plays classical music loudly on the stereo. Alex, who has been conditioned by Ludovico's Technique to become violently ill when hearing the music, attempts suicide by jumping out a window. He wakes up in the hospital badly injured. The suicide attempt leads government scientists to remove Ludovico's clockwork from Alex's brain. In an ironic reversal, F. Alexander is himself imprisoned for his actions and Alex is made a hero.

Alex's Parents

Alex's parents, whom Alex sometimes refers to as "pee and em," are passive though decent people. They behave in loving, if stereotypical, ways. His mother, for example, prepares meals for him to have when he returns from his adventures. They are afraid of Alex, though, and show no interest in knowing what he really does when he goes out with his friends. Although they do not take him back when he is released from prison, their interest in Alex returns after his suicide attempt and after the newspapers run stories about how he is a victim of government repression.

Billyboy

Billyboy leads a rival gang with whom Alex and his droogs battle. In the first section, when Alex, Dim, Georgie, and Pete come across Billyboy and his thugs attempting to rape a young girl in a warehouse, Alex's gang routs them. Billyboy's ugliness upsets Alex's aesthetic sensibility. Alex says of him: "Billyboy was something that made me want to sick just to viddy [see] his fat grinning litso [face]." In their new capacity as police, Billyboy and Georgie beat up Alex after he is released from prison and leave him for dead.

Dr. Branom

Dr. Branom works with Dr. Brodsky to rid Alex of his free will and humanity through Ludovico's Technique. He is friendly but insincere.

Dr. Brodsky

Dr. Brodsky is the psychologist in charge of administering Ludovico's Technique on Alex. He is a hypocrite and in many ways morally worse than Alex. He is a philistine of sorts, knowing nothing about music, which is, for Burgess, a "figure of celestial bliss." Materialist and scientist that he is, Brodsky considers music merely an "emotional heightener." He plainly takes pleasure in Alex's misery, laughing at the pain he experiences during the treatment. Before Alex is released from prison, Brodsky demonstrates to state and prison officials how Ludovico's Technique has turned Alex into a "true Christian."

D. B. daSilva

DaSilva is one of F. Alexander's liberal friends who helps him with Alex in the book's third section. Alex describes him as having effeminate behavior and a strong scent (aftershave or body odor).

P. R. Deltoid

Deltoid is Alex's state-appointed "Post-Corrective Advisor." He visits Alex after his night of ultraviolence in the novel's first section. Alex describes him as overworked and wearing a "filthy raincoat." Deltoid cannot understand why Alex, with a good home and parents, has turned out to be a juvenile delinquent. He visits Alex in jail and contemptuously spits in his face.

Dim

Dim is one of Alex's droogs. He is loud, brutish, stupid, and irritates Alex with his crassness and vulgarity. When Dim insults a woman singing opera at the Korova Milkbar, Alex punches him in the mouth, triggering the gang's resentment against Alex's tyrannical leadership. Alex also fights Dim the next day, cutting his wrist with a knife to show the gang that he is still the leader. By the novel's third section, Dim has joined the police force, along with Billyboy. The two of them rescue Alex, who is being attacked by a gang of old men, and take Alex to the country, where they beat him up and leave him for dead. As Burgess's characters are composites of Anglo and Russian youth culture, Dim could be read as an abbreviation for the Russian name, Dimitri.

Z. Dolin

Z. Dolin is one of F. Alexander's liberal friends who helps him with Alex in the novel's third section. Alex describes him as "a very wheezy smoky kind of veck" who is fat and sloppy, wears thick glasses, and chain smokes.

Georgie

Georgie is one of Alex's droogs, and second-in-charge. He attempts to take over the gang after Dim rebels against Alex at the Korova Milkbar, and leads the mutiny resulting in Alex's arrest at the end of the book's first section. More interested in money than violence per se, Georgie dies after being hit on the head by a man he and his droogs terrorize while Alex is in prison.

Joe

Joe is the boarder Alex's parents take in when Alex is sent to jail. Alex describes him as "a working-man type veck, very ugly, about thirty or forty." Joe has become a kind of surrogate son to Alex's parents, and he almost comes to blows with Alex when Alex comes home to see him eating eggs and toast with his parents.

Marty

Marty is one of the two ten-year-old girls that Alex picks up at the music store, plies with liquor, and rapes. He calls them "sophistos," meaning they are pretentious and try to act like adults. When the girls come to their senses and discover what Alex has done to them, they call him a "[b]east and hateful animal."

Minister of the Interior

The Minister of the Interior is a manipulative politician who symbolizes governmental repression and mindless bureaucracy. He chooses Alex—who refers to him as the "Minister of the Interior Inferior"—as a guinea pig for Ludovico's Technique, believing the treatment has the possibility to rid the country of undesirable elements. He turns Alex's attempted suicide to his favor by imprisoning F. Alexander, whom he describes as a "writer of subversive literature," and tricking Alex into a photo opportunity with him while Alex is still in the hospital. He wins Alex's favor by offering him a government job, a new stereo, and by playing Beethoven's Ninth Symphony for him.

Pete

Pete is the quietest of Alex's droogs, and the least questioning of his authority. In the last chapter, Alex runs into Pete and his wife. Pete now works for an insurance company and goes to harmless wine and scrabble parties at night, having given up his criminal ways. He represents maturity, and after seeing him, Alex begins thinking of marrying and settling down.

Prison Chaplain

The chaplain, a careerist and an alcoholic, befriends Alex in prison, permitting him to pick the music for services and listen to the stereo in chapel while reading the Bible. The chaplain finally speaks out against Ludovico's Technique when Alex is about to be released, arguing that human beings should be able to choose their actions. He is the character perhaps closest to Burgess's own philosophical position in the novel, and demonstrates this when he asks Alex, "What does God want? Does God want goodness or the choice of goodness? Is a man who chooses the bad perhaps in some way better than a man who has the good imposed upon him?" Alex, however, is clueless, and wants nothing more than to be released from prison. When the chaplain speaks out against the treatment in front of prison and state officials, he jeopardizes his own career.

Rex

Rex is a policeman and the driver who waits in the car, smoking and reading, while Billyboy and Dim beat Alex in the novel's third section.

Rubinstein

Rubinstein is one of F. Alexander's liberal friends who helps him with Alex in the third section of the novel. Alex describes him as "very tall and polite," and with an "eggy beard" (blonde).

Sonietta

Sonietta is one of the two ten-year-old girls that Alex rapes.

Themes

Free Will

A Clockwork Orange explores the ideas of good and evil by asking what it means to be human. Burgess asks and answers the question, "Is a man who has been forced to be good better than a man who chooses evil?" Alex chooses evil because it is in his nature to do so. His impulse towards good is artificial because it comes from outside of him, instilled by a government bent on controlling the populace by controlling their desires. By eliminating all of the bad in Alex through the Ludovico Technique, the government also eliminates that very thing that constitutes his humanity: his freedom to choose. They treat the symptom, not the cause of Alex's evil, oblivious of their own complicity in his behavior. For Burgess, an evil Alex is a human Alex and, hence, preferable to an Alex who has been programmed to deny his own nature. F. Alexander, the writer Alex and his droogs beat up, is one of the mouthpieces for this idea. At one point he says to Alex, "They have turned you into something other than a human being. You have no power of choice any longer. You are committed to socially acceptable acts, a little machine capable only of good." Later, he adds, "The essential intention [of the Ludovico Technique] is the real sin. A man who cannot choose ceases to be a man." The repetition of Alex's phrase "What's it going to be then, eh?" throughout the novel also underscores the theme of free will and individual choice.

Power

    A Clockwork Orange pits the intrusive powers of the state against the liberties of the individual. Burgess looks at the relationship between the state and the individual in a society that has deteriorated and is on the brink of anarchy. Left to its own devices, the state will attempt to control the individual through regulation, law, and brute force. This is evident in the manner in which Alex is used by the state as an example of its power to "rehabilitate" criminals. Rather than rehabilitate them, they reprogram them, brainwashing them. The cynical power-mongering of the state is embodied in the character of the Minister of the Interior, who manipulates Alex first into "volunteering" for the Ludovico Technique, and then into siding with the government after Alex's suicide attempt and return to his evil nature. A society in which the state has so much power, Burgess suggests, is one in which individual liberties such as freedom of speech and expression are crushed.

Topics for Further Study

- The setting for Burgess's novel is a dystopian society. What are some of its dystopic elements? Does the United States share any of these elements? Are there ways in which the United States can be described as a dystopia? Provide examples.

- Burgess claimed that *A Clockwork Orange* emphasizes the idea that free will is a central ingredient of what it means to be human. Write an essay agreeing or disagreeing with this notion and provide support for your argument from the novel.

- With your classmates, make a list of all the crimes that Alex and his droogs commit, then assign appropriate punishment for each crime. Be as specific as possible. On which items do you disagree with others in your group? What does this say about your own ideas of justice and the role of society in punishing criminals?

- With members of your class, draw up a list of slang terms or other words you use that older generations would not recognize. To what degree does using these words define your interaction with friends?

- Research the punishment for first-degree murder in your state. If possible, would you recommend that convicted murderers be given the opportunity to undergo the Ludovico Technique in lieu of the state sentence for murder? Why or why not? Explain if there are certain conditions you would attach.

- Research cases of political scandal in your own city or state and describe how that scandal is represented in newspaper or television accounts. How did the accused characterize their situation or their attackers? What does this tell you about the role of media in shaping public opinion?

- The Korova Milkbar symbolizes the decadence of Burgess's society in the novel. Name an analogous institution that symbolizes twenty-first-century American values and support your claim.

Selfhood

To fully grasp the human condition, Burgess implies in *A Clockwork Orange*, individuals must both recognize and accept their evil nature and recognize how society attempts to stifle it. Although Alex does not seem to understand the implications of the Ludovico Technique when it is initially explained to him, he does have an understanding of his own nature and how society has helped to form it. At one point he waxes philosophical, expressing an understanding of his "essential" self:

> More, badness is of the self, the one, the you or me on our oddy knockies [lonesome], and that self is made by old Bog or God and is his great pride and radosty [joy]. But the not-self cannot have the bad, meaning they of the government and the judges and the schools cannot allow the bad because they allow the self.

Alex knows he is evil, telling readers, "What I do I do because I like to do." The novel implies his degree of insight is greater than most people's insight. He accepts himself for who he is, rather than hiding behind illusions of what he should be according to others and the government. He experiences no guilt for his actions but embraces and revels in his evil side.

Morality

Burgess's moral universe in *A Clockwork Orange*, as in his other novels, can be described as a conflict between Augustinianism and Pelagianism. Augustinianism is derived from St. Augustine (354–430), who believed in humankind's innate depravity. Pelagianism is derived from Pelagius (c. 355–c. 425), whose doctrine held roughly that human beings were perfectible, and that evil was the result of superstition, social forces, the environment, and the like. In Burgess's novel, the government adhered to Pelagius-like thinking in that it tried to change human beings, to turn them away from their evil behavior through whatever means necessary. In Alex's case, it is the Ludovico Technique. Alex, who embraces his evil nature as if it were a second skin, chooses to be that way, but shows promise of choosing a different way in the book's final chapter, demonstrating that Burgess is not the consummate Augustinian that some critics have made him out to be. The tug between Augustinianism and Pelagianism creates the moral tension that sustains Alex's story, but it is a tension that remains largely unresolved.

Dystopia and Dystopian Ideas

A Clockwork Orange describes a dystopian

society. The opposite of utopias, or ideal societies, dystopias are severely malfunctioning societies. Dystopian novels such as George Orwell's *1984* portray bleak landscapes, corrupt social institutions, and characters among whom trust or authentic communication is impossible. The Korova Milkbar, where fifteen-year-olds can drink druglaced milk, symbolizes the decadence of the novel's setting, as does the fact that Alex—a charming rapist, killer, and thief—is the most appealing character in the story. Dystopian novels have a rich history and include works such as Jonathan Swift's eighteenth-century classic, *Gulliver's Travels*. However, they became especially prevalent and popular after World War II, as people increasingly took a dim view of human nature and the possibility for social change. Twentieth-century dystopian works include Aldous Huxley's *Brave New World*, Ayn Rand's *Atlas Shrugged*, and Ray Bradbury's *Fahrenheit 451*.

Style

Language

Nadsat, which means "teen" in Russian, is the language spoken in *A Clockwork Orange*. It is a mixture of Russian, English, and American slang, and rhyming words and phrases, with a touch of Shakespearean English. The singsong rhythm of the speech underscores the heavily stylized world of the novel and of Alex's own mind. Although many readers often initially struggle with understanding this slang of futuristic teenagers, they quickly pick up the speech patterns and the few hundred new words through the context in which they are used. By mirroring the violent acts the characters commit, Nadsat has a kind of onomatopoeic quality. That is, the words sound like the actions they describe. For example, "collocoll" means bell, and it also sounds like a bell ringing. Nadsat is also often highly metaphoric and ironic. The word "rabbit," for example, means to work, and the word "horrorshow" means beautiful. The former is metaphoric because working, for Alex, means engaging in meaningless and frenetic activity, which he associates with a rabbit's behavior. The latter is ironic because "horrorshow" suggests the opposite of what it means. Some of the words are just plain silly rhymes, reflecting a child's playful constructions. For example, "eggiwegg" for egg and "skolliwoll" for school.

Structure

The novel is divided into three sections of seven chapters each. In his introduction to the 1987 American edition of the novel, Burgess notes that "Novelists of my stamp are interested in what is called arithmology, meaning that [a] number has to mean something in human terms when they handle it." At twenty-one, citizens in Great Britain, the United States, and Russia can vote; the age symbolizes a mature human being. The novel is the story of one human being's growth into an adult, among other things.

1960s

In 1961, the year after Burgess had written his first draft of *A Clockwork Orange*, he and his wife took a trip to Leningrad (now St. Petersburg) in what was then the Soviet Union. During that trip, Burgess was appalled and intrigued by the roaming gangs of hoodlums he saw, called *stilyaqi*. Burgess noted how the police, preoccupied with ideological crimes against the state, had a difficult time controlling these unruly youths. He also noted the similarities of the Russian and British youth subcultures and was inspired to fashion a hooligan character who was a composite of the ways in which youth spoke, acted, and dressed in Russia and England.

Hence, Alex and his droogs—"droog" derived from the Russian word "drugi," which means "friends in violence." The stilyaqi, or style-boys, sprung up in Russia during the 1940s and were roughly contemporaneous with American beats. The stilyaqi listened to jazz and later to American rock and roll. The Soviet government considered them troublesome juveniles.

Compare & Contrast

- **1960s:** Following years of heated

protests and demonstrations, the United States passes the Civil Rights Act. The Act enforces the constitutional right to vote, guarantees relief against discrimination in public accommodations, and authorizes the Attorney General to initiate suits to protect constitutional rights in public facilities and public education.

Today: Some states have enacted hate crime legislation, which penalizes criminals for committing crimes based on a person's race, sexuality, religion, gender, ancestry, or national origin.

- **1960s:** The space race between the Soviet Union and the United States gathers momentum, as the Soviets send the first man into space to circle the earth, and the Americans land a man on the moon.

Today: The space race of the 1960s has given way to international cooperation to explore the heavens. Led by the United States, the International Space Station draws upon the scientific and technological resources of sixteen nations: Canada, Japan, Russia, eleven nations of the European Space Agency, and Brazil. Launch of the space station is set for 2004.

- **1960s:** The "Cold War" between the United States and the Soviet Union causes each country to be deeply suspicious of the other.

  Today: After the Soviet Union's dissolution, relations between Russia and the United States become warmer and more productive.

- **1960s:** The Beatles and the Rolling Stones gain international popularity and help shape the desires and tastes of youth culture.

  Today: The influence of rock and roll on contemporary youth is still strong, but other kinds of music such as techno, heavy metal, and world pop also exert strong influence.

The London youth subculture included groups known as teddyboys, mods, and rockers. Teddyboys emerged in the 1950s, as England was economically recovering from World War II and at the beginning of a consumer boom. Like many youth subcultures, they dressed to shock the status quo, wearing Edwardian-style drape jackets, suede Gibson shoes with thick crepe soles, narrow trousers, and loud ties. Like the greasers in movies such as *American Graffitti*, the teddyboys listened to rock and roll, fought rival gangs (often with razors and knives), and engaged in random vandalism. With the British popmusic boom of the 1960s, many teddyboys became rockers, wearing leather jackets, hanging out in working-class pubs, and riding motorcycles.

The mods, short for modernists, also emerged during the late 1950s in England. A more elitist group than the teddyboys, they wore their hair short; rode scooters; donned army anoraks; danced to groups such as the Creation, the Jam, and the Small Faces; and took amphetamines. The mods were sometimes referred to as "rude boys," and evolved into the "punks" and "skinheads" of the 1970s and later. For Burgess, however, being a mod, a stilyaqi, or a teddyboy, did not mean one practiced individual freedom. The trendy consumerism in which these group members engaged signaled a mindlessly slavish conformity.

Burgess also hated the control the state had over the individual, believing this control curtailed individual freedom. This state control was nowhere more evident than in the Soviet Union in the early 1960s, where Burgess saw firsthand the extent to which the communist government regulated the individual's life. Burgess especially detested the way in which communism shifted moral responsibility from the individual to the state. Though Britain was and is a democratic government, by the 1950s the Labour Party had nationalized many industries including coal (1946), electricity (1947), and the railways (1948). Also, in 1946, the National Health Service was founded to take care of British citizens' medical needs. This welfare state was odious to Burgess, who believed that it put the needs of society over the freedom of the individual.

Critical Overview

When *A Clockwork Orange* was published in 1962, it had twenty-one chapters. Its American edition, however, was published with only twenty chapters a year later, the publisher W. W. Norton having removed the last chapter because they thought it was too sentimental. It was not until 1987 that American editions were published with the last chapter included. Of the controversy, Burgess writes in his essay "*A Clockwork Orange* Resucked," found in the 1987 edition: "My book was Kennedyan and accepted the notion of moral progress. What was really wanted was a Nixonian book with no shred of optimism in it."

The reviews the novel received were generally favorable and emphasized both its thematic elements and its style. An anonymous reviewer for the *New York Times* calls the book "brilliant," and writes, "*A Clockwork Orange* is a tour-de-force in nastiness, an inventive primer in total violence, a savage satire on the distortions of the single and collective minds." The 1987 American edition carries a blurb from *Time* magazine which states, "Anthony Burgess has written what looks like a nasty little shocker, but is really that rare thing in English letters—a philosophical novel."

The novel has received its share of attention from academic critics as well. John W. Tilton, writing in *Cosmic Satire in the Contemporary*

Novel, praises Burgess's use of Nadsat, saying that Burgess used it "[t]o assure the survival of the novel by creating a slang idiom for Alex that would not grow stale or outmoded as real slang does." In his study of Burgess's novels entitled *The Clockwork Universe of Anthony Burgess*, critic Richard Mathews writes that "*A Clockwork Orange* is a masterpiece as both a novel and a film."

Comparing the kind of government in the novel to "a rotten mechanical fruit," Mathews argues that Alex's "disturbed spirit may somewhere awaken our sleeping moral sensibilities." Robert O. Evans, in his essay on Burgess in *British Novelists since 1900*, considers the work "an expression of disgust and revulsion about what has happened to society in our lifetimes." In her essay, "Linguistics, Mechanics, and Metaphysics: Anthony Burgess's *A Clockwork Orange*," Esther Petix writes, "The reader is as much a flailing victim of the author as he is a victim of time's finite presence." Petix notes that, like Alex, the reader also comes of age in reading the book, and "is charged with advancement and growth."

Sources

"Books of the Times," in *New York Times*, March 19, 1963.

Burgess, Anthony, *A Clockwork Orange*, Ballantine Books, 1988.

——————, *A Clockwork Orange*, W. W. Norton, 1987.

——————, "Introduction: *A Clockwork Orange* Resucked," in *A Clockwork Orange*, W. W. Norton, 1987.

——————, "On the Hopelessness of Turning Good Books into Films," in *New York Times*, April 20, 1975, pp. 14-15.

Coale, Samuel, *Anthony Burgess*, Frederick Ungar Publishing Co., 1981.

DeVitis, A. A., *Anthony Burgess*, Twayne Publishers, Inc., 1972.

Evans, Robert O., "The Nouveau Roman, Russian Dystopias, and Anthony Burgess," in *British Novelists Since 1900*, edited by Jack I. Biles, AMS Press, 1987, pp. 253-66.

Mathews, Richard, *The Clockwork Universe of Anthony Burgess*, The Borgo Press, 1978.

Petix, Esther, "Linguistics, Mechanics, and Metaphysics: Anthony Burgess's *A Clockwork Orange*," in *Critical Essays on Anthony Burgess*, edited by Geoffrey Aggeler, G. K. Hall, 1986, pp. 121-31.

Rabinovitz, Rubin, "Ethical Values in Burgess's *A Clockwork Orange*," in *Studies in the Novel*, Vol. 11, No. 1, Spring, 1979, pp. 43-50.

——————, "Mechanism vs. Organism: Anthony Burgess' *A Clockwork Orange*," in *Modern Fiction Studies*, Vol. 24, No. 4, Winter 1978, pp. 538-41.

Stinson, John J., *Anthony Burgess Revisited*, Twayne Publishers, 1991.

Tilton, John, *Cosmic Satire in the Contemporary Novel*, Bucknell University Press, 1977.

Further Reading

Aggeler, Geoffrey, *Anthony Burgess: The Artist as Novelist*, University of Alabama Press, 1979.

> Aggeler examines Burgess's books thematically. Burgess read and commented on Aggeler's book as it was being written.

Burgess, Anthony, *Little Wilson and Big God*, Weidenfeld & Nicolson, 1987.

> Burgess's autobiography is entertaining and illuminating, and well worth reading. He discusses his attitudes towards the reception both of his novel, *A Clockwork Orange*, and its film adaptation.

Hammer, Stephanie Barbe, "Conclusion: Resistance, Metaphysics, and the Aesthetics of Failure in Modern Criminal Literature," in *The Sublime Crime: Fascination, Failure and Form in Literature of the Enlightenment*, Southern Illinois University Press, 1994, pp. 154-74.

> Hammer discusses *A Clockwork Orange* as an example of criminal literature.

Pritchard, William H., "The Novels of Anthony Burgess," in *Massachusetts Review*, Vol. 7, No. 3. Summer 1996.

Pritchard explores the reader's feelings towards Alex and notes the novel's ability to almost make the reader feel relieved when Alex returns to his violent self.

Tilton, John, *Cosmic Satire in the Contemporary Novel*, Bucknell University Press, 1977.

Tilton's chapter on *A Clockwork Orange* explores the novel's main theme of free choice and suggests that Alex illustrates the belief that moral oppression violates individual civil rights as well as spiritual existence.

CPSIA information can be obtained
at www.ICGtesting.com
Printed in the USA
BVHW041346170919
558653BV00015B/396/P